POETRY ADVENTURES

I Saw an INVISIBLE LION TODAY

QUATRAINS

BRIAN P. CLEARY

ILLUSTRATIONS BY
RICHARD WATSON

Ⓜ MILLBROOK PRESS/MINNEAPOLIS

in Memory of
Paul "Pap" Collins
—B.P.C.

For Cat
—R.W.

Millbrook Press
A division of Lerner Publishing Group, Inc.
241 First Avenue North
Minneapolis, MN 55401 USA

For reading levels and more information, look up this title at www.lernerbooks.com.

Main body text set in Klepto ITC Std Regular 15/20.
Typeface provided by International Typeface Corp.

Library of Congress Cataloging-in-Publication Data

Names: Cleary, Brian P., 1959–
   Title: I saw an invisible lion today : quatrains / Brian P. Cleary.
   Description: Minneapolis, MN : Millbrook Press, [2016] | Series: Poetry
      adventures
   Identifiers: LCCN 2015013418| ISBN 9781467793421 (lb : alk. paper) | ISBN
      9781467797313 (pb : alk. paper) | ISBN 9781467797320 (eb pdf)
   Classification: LCC PS3553.L39144 A6 2016b | DDC 811/.54—dc23

LC record available at http://lccn.loc.gov/2015013418

Manufactured in the United States of America
2-45437-20295-2/21/2018

TABLE OF CONTENTS

WHaT ARe QuaTRaiNS?

Quatrains are four-line verses that usually rhyme. A quatrain might be just a single stanza (that's basically a "paragraph" of poetry) in a longer poem. Or it could be the entire poem. Quatrains come in twelve possible rhyme schemes, or patterns. These are the most common types: AAAA, AABB, ABCB, and ABAB.

In an AAAA rhyme scheme, all four lines will end with words that rhyme with one another, like *cat, bat, hat,* and *that.* Simple, right?

In AABB poems, the first two lines rhyme with each other—for example, *dog* and *frog.* The next two lines will rhyme with each other, but not with the first two, as in *pen* and *hen.*

The lines of an ABAB poem rhyme on alternating lines (every other line). Lines 1 and 3 rhyme with each other, and lines 2 and 4 rhyme with each other. That sounds really complicated, but here's an example of this rhyme scheme in a poem about quadruplets:

Matthew was born at ten twenty-seven;   (A)
And Molly, at ten thirty-four   (B)
Brendan was born at a half past eleven,   (A)
and Connor arrived just before.   (B)

Do you see how lines 1 and 3 (the A lines) rhyme with each other, and lines 2 and 4 (the B lines) also rhyme with each other, but not with the other lines? An ABAB rhyme scheme is as simple as that.

In this book, you'll also find examples of an ABCB rhyme scheme. in this pattern, lines 2 and 4 in each stanza rhyme with each other, but the other lines don't rhyme.

Don't think of these rhyme schemes as *rules*—think of them more as *options*. Pick a topic and tell your story in whatever rhyming pattern you choose. Have fun with your rhyming and with your poems!

I saw an INVISiBLE LiON TODaY

rhyme scheme: ABCB

I saw an invisible lion today
and fourteen invisible leopards.
And thirty invisible sheep being led
by seven invisible shepherds.

I saw an invisible baby giraffe
who ate from invisible trees.
I watched as he shook an invisible nest
that was filled with invisible bees.

I saw an invisible penguin who skated
upon an invisible rink
along with a group of invisible skunks
who had made an invisible stink.

I saw an invisible clown who was juggling
three highly invisible balls
as he jumped back and forth on invisible horses
running out of invisible stalls.

I saw an invisible witch as she cackled
atop her invisible broom.
It's pretty amazing the things that I saw—
without ever leaving my room.

It's Raining Adjectives

rhyme scheme: ABCB

Hey, look! It's raining adjectives!
It's pouring plain and fancy.
It's dripping dark and dangerous,
Mysterious and chancy.

My hat is drenched in jubilant.
The puddles pop with jumpy.
My socks are soaked with squishy, stinky,
soggy, soft, and lumpy.

8

The gutter's overflowing too
with spooky, strange, and sneaky.
The drain is backing up with loaded,
laughable, and leaky.

It's coming down with clamorous,
cantankerous, and clunky.
It's splattering, splendiferous,
fantabulous, and funky.

The weatherman looks skyward,
as he shouts, "What's up? What gives?
It isn't raining cats and dogs—
it's raining adjectives!"

I CAN'T FIND MY THESAURUS

rhyme scheme: ABCB

I can't find my thesaurus.
I'm really quite disturbed,
aggravated, agitated,
angry, and perturbed.

Whoever came and borrowed it,
return it straightaway,
instantly, directly—
right this minute! Now!! Today!!!

MY FATHER'S MUSTACHE

rhyme scheme: ABCB

My father's mustache is the largest in town.
It's bigger than all of the others.
It grows all along the width of his face
and continues right onto his brother's.

SLEEPOVER PARTY

rhyme scheme: ABCB

The letters had a sleepover
with popcorn, snacks, and TV.
But drinking too much soda
Made the elemeno *P*.

I've Done (Almost) Everything
rhyme scheme: ABCB

I speak about a dozen different languages.
I've won all thirteen marathons I've run.
I've written several superhero comic books,
invented both the hot dog and the bun.

I coined the phrase, "What's up?" when I was seven.
I once flew back in time to see Babe Ruth.
I struck him out in three—yes, it's amazing being me.
I've done everything, except, well . . . tell the truth.

ON OPPOSITE DAY

rhyme scheme: ABCB

On opposite day when up is down
and organized is messy,
off means on and in means out
and casual is dressy.

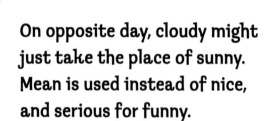

On opposite day, cloudy might
just take the place of sunny.
Mean is used instead of nice,
and serious for funny.

If on this day when happy's sad
and awesome means unbearable,
your mom makes you your favorite soup,
just slurp and say, "That's terrible."

It's Grandma

rhyme scheme: AAAA

How to untangle a kinked-up hose?
Count to nineteen without using your toes?
Get pizza sauce out of your picture-day clothes?
You know who knows? Grandma knows.

Comes up with nicknames like Schnookums and Fuzz?
Knows the best lullaby there ever was?
Gives you a favorite treat . . . just because?
You know who does? Grandma does.

THeRe's a ReasON I'M AsKiNG

rhyme scheme: ABAB

What insect has eleven teeth,
is furry and oozing and black?
Has horns and a tail, some scabs underneath?
I don't know, but there's one on your back!

IT COULD BE WORSE

rhyme scheme: ABCB

Cleaning the litter box, scooping and sifting,
I gag as I whisper a vow:
I'll never ask my mother or dad
if I can adopt a pet cow.

HOME

rhyme scheme: AABB

I went to school in Paris. I went to school in Turkey.
A half a year in London, Omaha, and Albuquerque.
I went to school in China, New Delhi, and in Guam,
and for a little while, I went to school in Vietnam.

I went to school in Sicily; then after that, Sri Lanka.
I spent a very chilly wintertime in Minnetonka.
I went to school in Amsterdam, in Hamburg, and in Rome.
As long as I had books with me, I always felt at home.

MY NeiGHBORS HaVe GOT a PeT RHiNO

rhyme scheme: ABCB

My neighbors have got a pet rhino
who hasn't a horn on its head.
Just a wee little nose, two baby blue eyes,
and a soft set of whiskers instead.

She's nowhere as big as the ones at the zoo.
She's downy and furry and fluffy.
She'll meow and she'll purr as she licks at her fur.
I love their rhinoceros, Muffy.

AT THE SHORE

rhyme scheme: AABB

Deep in the summertime, late in the day,
the salt water laps at the pier by the bay.
A sliver above throws a wink of moonlight.
The wind in the willow trees whispers good night.

You're Supposed To Be You

rhyme scheme: ABAB

You're supposed to be you—
it's kind of your job.
You're not to be Lou
or Mackenzie or Bob.

You're not to be Mary
or Michael or Sue.
You're not to be Harry
or Lizzy but you.

If you're somebody else,
then there will be two
of that somebody else
but zero of you.

HELLO, MY NAME IS

Me!

RHYME TIME

rhyme scheme: ABAB

I wrote up a list of some rhymes for my verse
And hoped I could use "Madagascar."
I just cannot rhyme it—each time it was worse,
So I guess I'll just go watch some NASCAR.

OH, WAIT!

rhyme scheme: ABCB

I have to write a four-line poem
that rhymes lines 4 and 2.
There's no way I can finish it.
Today's the day it's due!

QUATRAIN FOR A TOT TRAIN

rhyme scheme: AABB

I got myself a tiny train for back and forth to school.
Instead of coal, I shovel chocolate chips to burn for fuel.
My engine pulls eleven cars and one bright red caboose,
with room for all my snacks and stuff, like PBJs and juice.

Although it's just a little train, its whistle's loud and whiny,
and all the seats are plenty big for any tot-sized hiney.
With overalls and pocket watch and cap, it's pretty cool
to be the pint-sized engineer who takes the tots to school.

SUMMER CAMP

rhyme scheme: ABCB

It's snowing fireflies in June,
marshmallows oozing from the s'mores,
crickets swapping late-night tales—
perfection in the out of doors.

THINK AGAIN
rhyme scheme: ABCB

The toothbrush said, "My job here sure is filthy."
The sink responded, "I've got people spitting
inside me every day. I've got the grossest job—okay?"
The toilet answered both, "You must be kidding."

MY Least Favorite Things

rhyme scheme: AABB

Homework and paper cuts, chores and big blisters,
sharing a room with my two younger sisters,
brown, muddy puddles beneath all the swings—
these are a bunch of my least favorite things.

ALMOST EVERYONE

rhyme scheme: ABCB

My birthday was great—we had music and cake
and a forty-two-inch enchilada.
With gifts, games, and ice cream, we all had some fun.
Well . . . everyone but the piñata.

AT THE MUZZALOO STORE

rhyme scheme: AABB

At the muzzaloo store, there are crates of persnoobles,
fresh-baked flobitzen and tazbees with jubles.
They're stocking the shelves with the best alaprises,
Ungden, and traffadoo (three different sizes!).

High on the shelf, you'll find mezeloid dinkles—
the nice, silky, smooth kind without any wrinkles.
Jars filled with tomashes and wazzenloft too.
Boxes of mooglehorns, yellow and blue.

Right down aisle 7 is where they keep japers—
stacked and wrapped neatly in pink tissue papers—
mozenar, trums, castanoovas, and more:
you'll find all of these at the muzzaloo store!

FURTHER READING

BOOKS

Hoose, Phillip M. *Hey, Little Ant*. Berkeley, CA: Tricycle, 1998.
Want to see how quatrains can be used in a book? *Hey, Little Ant* is a story about a boy and his encounter with an ant—and it's all written in quatrains!

Kalz, Jill, comp. *Tickles, Pickles, and Floofing Persnickles: Reading and Writing Nonsense Poems*. North Mankato, MN: Picture Window Books, 2014.
Check out examples of nonsense poems, similar to "At the Muzaloo Store" in this book, and get tips about how to write your own.

Prelutsky, Jack. *Pizza, Pigs, and Poetry: How to Write a Poem*. New York: Greenwillow, 2008.
Would you like to write your own poetry? Here are some expert tips for turning your own experiences and stories about your family, your pets, and your friends into poems.

WEBSITES

Quatrains! Get Your Quatrains Here!
http://www.poemfarm.amylv.com/2011/04/quatrains-get-your-quatrains-here.html
Explore the website of children's author Amy Ludwig VanDerwater and learn all about quatrains! Sample poems and easy rhyming instructions can also be found here.

RhymeZone
http://www.rhymezone.com/
Use this website to find words that rhyme so you can create your own quatrains.

Writing Forward
http://www.writingforward.com/writing_exercises/creative-writing-exercises /from-101-creative-writing-exercises-couplets-and-quatrains
Follow tips to create your own quatrains. Writing prompts and sample topics are also included.